A remarkable c_____ _____ victory over life's challenges as Emete boldly declares Christ's glory as the final destination for those who accept the open and warm invitation to jump in and receive him.

Veronica Ikechi, Mind Coach, Speaker, Kingdom Walkers Ministry

Here is a collection of poetry about the discovery of faith in all phases in our lives. Wherever we may find ourselves, we acknowledge and celebrate through poetic utterance and expressions.

Uzo Ojinnaka, Poet

Inspired for Purpose is a must-have! As I read, it really speaks to some circumstances in my own life, giving me a picture of what the other side will look like. I also like the fact that the poems really relate to the suffering of life but at the same time brings out hope of the victories and breakthroughs! Amongst my favourites are "I don't look like what I've been through" and "Life after Redundancy".

Swabrina Love, Femininity and Healing Coach

The author has employed a variety of literary/ poetry tools to bring home the message of resilience, strength and trust in God as we see, and work through, the weaknesses and failings of humanity.

The use of free verses, relatable imagery and metaphors and references to bible verses in a way that engages rather than alienates makes the work open and inclusive. As a result, it not hard to determine the essential theme of these poems, and how Godly faith will help ride the storms and vicissitudes of life.

In Phase 1, The Challenges of Life, the use of enjambments in these free verse poem works well in keeping readers engaged with the poet's thoughts and words as expressed in her writing.

It's Raining, it's Storming uses relatable and everyday occurrences that the reader can very well empathise with and relate to. With an irregular rhyme scheme, the author demonstrates the chaotic sequence of events with one mishap after the other in an ever increasing and overwhelming run of events.

Eric Ayoola (BSc.LLB), Head of Strategy and Performance with a London Borough

INSPIRED *for* PURPOSE

Rhymes and Rhythms

Copyright © 2024 Emete Ogbomo

The moral right of the author has been asserted.

Apart from any fair dealing for the purposes of research or private study, or criticism or review, as permitted under Copyright, Design and Patents Act 1998, this publication may only be reproduced, stored or transmitted, in any form or by any means, with prior permission in writing of the publishers, or in any case of the reprographic reproduction in accordance with the terms of licences issued by the Copyright Licensing Agency. Enquiries concerning reproduction outside these terms should be sent to the publishers.

PublishU Ltd
www.PublishU.com

Scripture from the Holy Bible, New International Version®, NIV®. Copyright © 1973, 1978, 1984, 2011 by Biblica, Inc.™ Used by permission of Zondervan.
All rights reserved worldwide.

All rights of this publication are reserved.

Dedication

This book is dedicated to my late Mother Mrs Comfort Ogbomo, born on 1 December 1937 and passed away on 23 August 2021.

Throughout her adult life, Comfort emulated and demonstrated her name, regardless of life's challenges her qualities remained the same. She comforted many with good deeds and loving care, tirelessly active in cultural community affairs. Retirement in her 60s was no restriction to her active social exploits, no limitation to sharing her opinion in community meetings as a respected voice.

A wife, mother-of-five and despite no formal education, she progressed in life and thrived; she is remembered for many good things including her smile. A conscientious seamstress into her final days, colourful fabrics filled her wardrobe and draws to be worn in a variety of ways.

Comfort, Comfort, a mother held dear to all who knew her, forever in our hearts passed from this earth into eternal peace forever. She is remembered for good, remembered with love and the assured hope of being reunited in the future Heaven above.

Thanks

My thanks and appreciation go to my Dad
Francis Ogbomo, my niece, brother and sisters
for supporting and cheering me on
this poetically inspired journey.

Also, to the many friends and supporters who
also played a part, through encouraging
words that warm and gladden the heart!

Special thanks and appreciation go to Uzo Ojinnaka,
Veronica Ikechi, Eric Ayoola and Swabrina Love,
who extended me their time in reviewing my
draft and provided extensive, honest, and very
useful feedback. Your input was encouraging
and contributed to the refinement of the
contents of the book.

Contents

Dedication & Thanks

Phase 1:
The Challenges of Life

Phase 2:
The Whole World is a Stage

Phase 3:
Radical Love

Phase 4:
The Beauty of Salvation

Phase 5:
The Wonders of Faith

Phase 6:
Kingdom Living

Phase 7:
Affirmation Time
"I am" Statements of Truth

About the Author

EMETE OGBOMO

Introduction

This journey began just a few years ago with encouraging words I heard, "The best is yet to come."

Over the years since February 1996, I often found myself paused with a pen writing poetic words, as I took time to reflect on the state of my personal affairs, social and emotional ups and downs, interspersed with life's various cares.

Often when observing current affairs, my heart and mind were stirred to poetic despair, the state of the Nations far and wide, social upheaval, political unrest, terror, and much fear.

Then there are the seasons and cycles in life winter, spring, summer and without fail autumn time.

Alongside my legal profession, I found poetic expression for the various and manifold life experiences, digression from focus with bumps in the road, tippy on toes.

I would sit down and ponder life's circumstances, challenges social events and compose rhymes and rhythms, poetic discourses an expression of my mind's thoughts poetically voiced.

Poem after poem inscribed in a leather-bound book, I would often look over and comment, that's so real and encouraging words soften the woes are good.

I would question maybe others can benefit from the words in the book, so thoughts of purpose began to unfold. Lo and behold, whilst browsing the supermarket a year or so ago, I got speaking to a lady who was very chatty and at the same time bold. Are you an author she asked, I see you authoring poems and books in numbers quite vast.

Rhymes and Rhythms emerged about different seasons, in life with fuel-injected hope, the ability to cope with challenges, aiming at the finish line and the end goal of a brighter tomorrow.

So, Inspired for Purpose was birthed from the heartfelt human experiences in life, the best, unrehearsed sometimes the worst; however, undergirded by faith in God brings the warmth of a sunburst.

Enjoy the phases, embrace the encouragement and be Inspired for Purpose.

Phase 1

The Challenges of Life

EMETE OGBOMO

Along Life's Road

On our interesting journey along life's road,
we'll have experiences that might, sometimes,
land us in a place of despair;
a lack of hope questioning:
Does anyone really care?

Hope for the future, the good things in life,
weighed down by worries, challenges, cares,
bitterness and strife.

Amid the circumstances, we're unable to see
the wood for the trees; clouded by negative
thoughts encircling 360 degrees!

Despair and discouragement impacts adversely
on our ability, to move forward with expectancy,
the opportunity to embrace endless possibilities.
Anxiety is said to be an aunty to worry and fear,
that weighs on the mind reiterating
false evidence daily reappears.

God is mighty, so surrender all anxiety,
cast every care, relinquish the despair,
He'll push back the darkness and
flood your soul with loving care.

It's Raining, It's Storming

It's raining, it's storming for the last few months
my life has been less than boring!
It's raining, it's pouring I woke up one morning
unaware of the storm that was brewing.

It started with a stomach-ache
but ends with my God is so great!

It's raining, it's storming, I'm a bit under the weather
but should feel better in the morning.

Woke up in the morning seeking for breakfast,
the cooker's not working, oh, that's a first;
I've not much energy so for an electrician,
I start my search.

It's raining, it's storming, oh no, the overflow pipe
to the boiler is pouring; call the midwife
no I need a plumber, I'm not thinking straight,
and my stomach feels numb, so the drama began.

The plumber said I'm coming, I promise you I'm
coming, for three days the pipe overflowed,
my goodness it's raining, it's storming.

The fourth day came, the plumber's on his way,
I receive a phone call—oh there's been a delay,
he's knocked over a cyclist and the police are
on the way; an ambulance has taken the
injured man away, I can no longer come today!

It's raining, it's storming, glory hallelujah
joy's coming in the morning.

999/111 hurry, hurry, quick please come, there's pain
in my chest several places more than just one.
In my tears and distress, I didn't scream, I didn't
shout, I had every confidence in God that he
would work it all out.

Cardiologist, Consultant, Doctor and Nurse,
specialist equipment surround me;
could it be worse?

Give me a minute to rest my head on the
hospital bed, the mobile rings my heart goes ping
message from my neighbour; I can see tarpaulin
hanging loose from your roof, needs attending now,
if I tell you the truth.

Oh Lord, it's raining, it's storming this juncture
of my life is far from boring;
Yet, morning by morning God's new mercies I see,
surrounding, encompassing and bestowed upon me
according to Lamentations 3:23.

Pain, pain, chronic pain, the Doctor asks me on the
scale of one to ten what do you say? I answer
through tears its bad and needs to go away.
What heights of love, such depths of God's peace,
I was in such good hands and in a few days released.

Home, I went time to recoup, medication in hand and
equipped with God's Truth. Time to rest up in the
hands of the Man with the master plan.
Saviour, healer, shield and defence strong tower
and my best friend.

The prayers of friends I have to mention, went up to
God's ear and caught his attention.

After a couple of weeks, I'm stepping out, not going
too far, my battery's flat, oh no, someone's hit
my new car. They've cracked the bumper,
no note left and no number.

It's raining, it's storming, still I live in hope
as joy comes in the morning.
It's raining, it's storming from Heaven my God
comes a roaring!

Morning time comes where's the rain?
There're no dark clouds, no chronic pain, my
strength regained, heart and mouth exclaimed;
great is the Lord and greatly to be praised, who
never sleeps nor slumbers through the storm
but came to my aid.

The God on the mountain is the same God in the
valley moments of life he works supernaturally
to put things right.

It's raining, it's storming but a new day is dawning
in God's plan and purpose for my life.
The end of this rhyme I'm nearly there,
one truth and this I must share;
Throughout the storm, God did not give me
more than I could bear.

It's raining, it's storming, in partnership with God,
joy always comes in the morning!

The Journey from Down there to Up Here

The journey from down there to up here is not
without wear and tear; it's not without its challenges,
heartache pain and oftentimes despair!
The road can be long and oftentimes we fall short
of strong with bumps, twists and turns,
yet the heart yearns to push on and not quit.
I guess there's an inner knowing of what one can do,
despite the obstacles in the natural
presenting so real and so true.
But, somehow, somewhere a force from within
acts as a propelling wind, with the assurance that
success is attainable as we are all born to win.
I liken it to a call to purpose; to arise and shine
take hold of each moment in
different seasons and times.
I am who I am, you are who you are,
and a can-do attitude will take us far.
Thus far have I come and there's more to be done,
so on my morals do I not sit
but express gratitude for the past,
current and what's to come—a bit like
Joseph to the palace from the pit.
Be under no illusion, commitment, hard work
are all necessary applications.
The route to succeeding requires consistency,
dedication, persistence and vocation,
that builds character.

Oftentimes success in life comes with a price, a
mountain to climb, a valley to be raised,
achievements can come in diverse ways.
The journey from down there to up here
with life happening in between,
it's not as easy as it appears on the outside
as it seems.
You see me and I see you successful, achievers
and yes, life is good.
Of the many things that are sure, in aspiring higher,
I was never flawed by a no or closed door.
To believe that you can, may require
a re-routing of the plan.
Could it be that, for you and me,
the secret weapon is purpose,
our key to fulfilling destiny?
The journey from down there to up here
with life's inevitable, in-betweens,
the rivers to cross the mountains to climb
no matter how difficult it seems.
The journey from down there to up here is not
without its tears, sometimes for many years,
however, never give up on your dreams,
life goals or vision.
Keep your eyes on the prize and with this I surmise,
all things are possible for the one who believes.

How Many More, How Many More?

Text from friends throughout the night,
fire in West London a terrifying sight.
I sit, I sigh, I question, why, oh why?
tears well up on the verge to cry.

How many more, how many more,
can we really afford to ignore?

Bombings, fires, attacks of the terrorist kind,
stabbings, another youth dies more victims
of vicious knife crime.

Murders, wars, rumours of wars, famines, assaults,
earthquakes in diverse places, hundreds of lives
lost to cancer, political upheaval, hung parliaments
and so much more.

What's the score is God being ignored?
He cannot be ignored for it is written, [Romans 1:19],
God has made himself known, in all that has been
created and can be seen.
The mountain top to the beautiful lush green valleys
in different locations across the pond
throughout the nations.

Can't you see the magnitude of the need,
recognise the flaw, the open door
of broken humanity, consumed with greed,
personal need, me and mine for others
outside my circle I have no time.

Call on God, acknowledge the one with the
master plan who holds the keys to our lives
in his Almighty hands.

He foresaw fallen humanity's need
and sent his seed into a woman.
Mary blessed Mary, chosen to carry a special baby.
Jesus Christ is his name, salvation is his aim, for all
who call on him, he will never turn away.

The unbelieving heart, young people set apart,
families and relations all included have
an appointment a daily chance
for a brand-new start!

How many more, how many more;
can you really afford to ignore?

I Don't Look Like What I've Been Through

I don't look like what I've been through:
the heartache and the pain, internal struggles the
undoing of a couple, the stress and ensuing strain.

I don't look like what I've been through
despite what your eyes can see,
the emotional rollercoaster fighting the battles of life
that confronted me on every side and that daily.

I don't look like what I've been through
in the days, weeks, months and years gone by,
but I can say each and every day
the good Lord heard my cry.

My cry for help, my cry for mercy in desperation,
never once did the Lord not hear me.

The journey was long, the battle was fierce, for
every one of my scars Jesus Christ was pierced.
From victim to victor, I emerged unscathed,
equipped with experience for the rest of my days.

Although I faltered and waivered in faith, by his grace
I remained steadfast in seeking God's face
and waited for the Lord's hand to come through
for me, this he did and set me free.

From the fear of the enemy, anxiety, depression
and much more, he broke the chains that held me
bound and set before me an open door.

The pathway to freedom the pathway of life,
freedom from turmoil, freedom from strife.

Striving within and the enemy of sin, the deep valleys
bought up and the mountains made plain.

I don't look like what I've been through
I'm telling you the truth, the anguish from abuse,
the days, the mornings, the afternoons, the evenings
when I screamed and shouted from the roof.

I don't look like what I've been through,
when my friends were not around, the enemy
encroaching on every side like dogs
a pack of ferocious hounds.

I don't look like what I've been through,
the battles that I faced each day,
the scars of which and internal turmoil
have all been washed away.

I don't look like what I've been through,
how come I hear you say, the internal battles
the daily struggles have all but faded away.

I don't look like what I've been through
in journeying through the valley of the shadow
of death, God was with me through the tears,
the days beside myself, bereft.

I don't look like what I've been through,
and I've lived to tell the tale, the days bereft
beside me, the stormy wintry gales.

I don't look like what I've been through,
with no desire to revisit it again,
I nearly lost my mind bordering on insane.

I don't look like what I've been through,
the lies, deceit, the promises relinquished on;
bleat, bleat like a lost sheep.

I don't look like what I've been through
how's that I hear you ask, the Love of God
came rushing in and healed my broken heart,
my bruises and internal scars.

I don't look like what I've been through,
I pause for you to think... As you do,
I invite you to the River of Life to drink.

INSPIRED FOR PURPOSE

Life After Redundancy

Hear me when I say, there is life after redundancy,
hear me when I say there is life after redundancy!

God, you see, had a plan for me, before time began
—my life was in his hands.
My pathway purposed by his decree, so
non-appointments to jobs, positions and roles
were only signposts of the future
he destined for me.

I waited with hope, expectant anticipation,
to see the beauty and fullness of his plans unfold
for me the next steps to elevation.
Before my very eyes, sometimes with tears and cries,
but that's okay
for he leads the way, as I recall in Psalm 23 it does
say, "In paths of righteousness he leads me.'

Redundancy, redundancy now I see, the purpose
God had and how it served to propel
and advance me.
It was just for a season, a moment in time God,
Jehovah-Jireh provided and he's always on time.

Far beyond that season and moment in time,
lay his plans for a new future brimming with
hope and his love, so divine.

Darkened corridors swing open wide, glory to God
who does not swerve from his promise to provide.

So here I am on the other side of redundancy,
enriched, blessed, lacking nothing and so grateful
and full of abundancy.

It was to my gain ... redundancy that is,
as I can testify of the fruit of God's divine will.
Spiritual maturity, financial stability, business
opportunity and no more social security!

A new job and much joy, peace and hope
faith within and a renewed vigour
to serve my creator, my King.
So, you see, life in Christ continues
and is so much sweeter after redundancy.

The Times We're In!

The times we're in are perilous,
the times we're in are hard.
Fear, anxiety, desperation all around
broken people, marred and scarred
depression daily knocking at the door.
Increased petrol prices, national insurance
contributions, essential utilities and the like
with little or no concessions.
Help, help the people cry,
the government needs to do something,
we can no longer afford to buy
the essentials for life, the prices are so hiked.
So, what's the response to the ever-increasing
financial crunch?
What do we do, what can be done?
Let's lift our eyes to the skies,
that's where the help comes from,
God above and beyond; the all-sufficient one.

"Whatever May Come, Whatever May Go"

Whatever may come, whatever may go,
one thing is sure,
God's Word remains unchanged,
established in Heaven and it is just so!
Whatever may come, whatever may go,
God knows tomorrow
And his purpose for our lives is unflawed.

Whatever may come, whatever may go,
God's love remains constant,
an ever-flowing stream up on the high mountain
flowing deep in the valley below.
Whatever may come, whatever may go,
the signs of the times, the end of the age
is pre-determined and evident all around us,
as we come and as we go.

Whatever may come, whatever may go,
know this, the presence of God's Spirit is as an
ever-present glow.
No display of the flesh, no evidence of hate,
no show of carnality or any of that,
just peace, love and purity settled and wrapped
in God's power that flows.

So, whatever may come, whatever may go,
forever God will reign,
And His kingdom is manifested,
His purpose fulfilled,
His Word comes to pass,
and His children advance
in His power, a sight to behold.

Whatever may come and whatever may go,
know that God was,
God is and still to come again.
Whatever may come and whatever may go!

Sandra, A Life Lived

Sandra, a life lost but a life lived.
A life lived, given over to God
and serving others in love.
Tirelessly, sacrificially, earnestly, wholeheartedly,
willingly, consistently and compassionately.
A life lived not for me, mine, my own
but given to the owner and lover of her soul,
The captain of her salvation to whom
she has since gone home.
Heaven, the resting place of the saints,
the gates await those who believe in God
And receive him through His son Jesus Christ,
the Saviour of the world.
A life given, a life lived, a life called home,
a life lived on purpose connected to God's throne.
All thanks to God for Sandra's life
and a whole lot more.
Will you open the door of your heart and let him in?
He'll clean you up and deliver you from sin that lies
deep within the recesses of our hearts.
It was not so from the start but through human sin,
God's Spirit did depart.
Adam, God called wherefore thou art?
Are you hiding, hiding from God in the guise of
I'm okay, I'm doing all right?

He sees, he hears the cries of your heart,
desperately seeking the answers to it all
Why am I down? Why am I brown?
Why I am sick? Why do I nick?
Why am I so quick to speak evil and why
at the sight of trouble I don't even quibble?

Answers, answers, humans seek answers,
Jesus said:
I am the Way, I am the Truth, I am the Life,
no one can access the Creator God except to
come through me, call on me, call to me, come to me
all you who labour and are heavily laden with;
Woes, troubles, trials, temptations, tribulations, pains
and no gain from your labour and I will give you rest
for your weary soul [John 14:6 and Matthew 11:28].
Like Sandra, a life lost but a lived-in relationship
with the Creator of it all.

Life's Display

There they go, day by day,
many hundreds, thousands pass by this way,
from the outside they seem to look okay.
A crooked smile, a prideful look,
question is your name written in the book?
The book of life through Jesus Christ,
only a few passes there from death to life.

Wide for destruction and broad is the gate,
the devil's pathway that's doomed,
As a result, we will all give an account
at the pearly gates. [Matthew 7:13]

Jesus Christ said come unto me all of you
that are weary, heavily weighed down and poor,
I will give you rest, new life and
so much more. [Matthew 11:28]

Choices

Choices, choices this life if full of choices,
the freedom to choose what you want to do.
The freedom to choose what path to take:
left or right or whether to go straight.
The choice to work while it is day, sleep throughout
the night, waste away time in fun, frivolity and play.
Choices, choices, sometimes in deciding which way
to go, there are competing voices affecting
which choice is the best leading to
rejoicing and nothing less.
In the Good Book we see the narrow path leads
to eternal life, those who find it are few
and far between. [Matthew 7:13-14]
Yet, wide is the path leading to destruction,
so many choose this with
unfortunate consequences.
Choose a Life with Jesus Christ and be destined
for higher heights propelled into purpose,
No winging it but a divine spring in your step and
no regret, purposed by design specific
Kairos moments seasons and times.
Carpe diem—seize the moment and time,
take hold of the Man with the master plan,
The Creator of all humanity, go forward, exceed,
fulfil purpose and achieve destiny at God's speed
choose life and this is a guarantee.

The Challenges of Life

The challenges of Life, incidents, accidents monetary
madness, badness, sadness, people are callous.
Holding malice, rudeness no goodness, the
tendency for strife, husband and wife,
affliction from a crisis midlife,
tossing and turning throughout the night
like the sides of dice, the challenges of life!
Each and every day challenges can present
themselves in a manifold and diversity of ways,
not quite sure what's going to take place.
Will I be up today and down tomorrow,
will my heart be broken in love, will I suffer
bereavement and much sorrow?
Morning is dawning and the news of another life
taken, child molestation, disease breakout
hits another nation.
The challenges of life confronts every man, boy,
woman and child.
Every race and nationality, colour and creed, none
passes under the radar of challenges to meet.
The challenges of life, battling through the forest
of our thoughts, wading through the messiness of
our minds, negative attitudes, cares and burdens
weighing heavy on every side.
Financial, emotional, social and political, a range
a host a daily dose of the challenges of life.
Counselling, therapy talking helplines alike,
sources to manage the challenges of life.

Prayer For You

Dear God, here I am to share
the Good News of the Gospel to all in despair.

Desperation of heart, mind body and soul
draw them unto you through your son
Jesus Christ and make them whole.

Don't Give Up

Don't give up on hope, don't give up on faith,
don't give up the dream, no matter
how hard life seems.

Life, A Precious Gift

Our lives are precious,
every life has intrinsic value.
The measure of life consists
of what we contribute to humanity
making a difference in our spheres
of influence and in all that we do.

It's Alright, It's Okay

It's all right, it's okay tomorrow
always brings a brighter day.
God's mercies come my way
new every morning abounding
resounding with his
goodness displayed.

EMETE OGBOMO

Phase 2

The World Stage

The World is Quaking, God is Shaking

There's no mistaking the whole World is quaking,
God is shaking.
Shaking up and shaking down,
God is shaking things all around.
People, places, nations, churches, celebrity
preachers and fake Bible teachers.
Leaders to the left, right, centre, all shades and
colours social, political, ethical and moral.
Where do you stand? Quick dry or sinking sand?
Whatever the quaking, whatever the shaking,
God is making a way through the wilderness of life,
highways through the desert.
Extending mercy in the face of judgment,
mercy and grace in great multitude
in every nation,
in every place.
The world is quaking, God is making
all things new
for me and for you.

The Whole World is a Stage

The whole World is a stage, we all are actors and
with roles to play, scripted for each and every day.
An opportunity for a fresh start, a blank page!
To arise and shine in different seasons and times,
the young, middle age, elders,
and those in their prime.
Seize the moment in moving forward so we all climb.
We all have the chance to be and become;
a trailblazer, world changer, lifesaver,
pacesetter, destiny maker,
the best version of you in all that you do
and that's the truth!
Procrastination, the thief of time, reservations
trouble the mind, fear and doubt lurking about.
Step out, move forward, act by faith
and remember the say,
Rome, dear friend, was not built in a day!

EMETE OGBOMO

We All Have a Battle to Fight!

Wars, wars and rumours of wars,
we all have a battle to fight, a river to cross—
I have my story what's yours?

Just as life is a journey and the whole world is a
stage some seasons in life come
with a battle to wage.

As we turn the page of a new year, there will be
challenges ups and downs, swings and roundabout.
Watch out for the kerb, sometimes it feels like we're
on the verge of losing it all, taking a fall, guess what,
life just threw us a curve ball.

Consider the plight of the poor, the unloved,
the widow and lonely. We all have a battle to fight
during the daylight hours and at times
throughout the night.
I am aware of a brighter tomorrow, no fears no pain
heartache or sorrow no anxious feelings
in my soul so hollow.

How can that be? How can I see a brighter future
for my family; where is that place for me and my
family to make haste?

Come, go with me to Calvary;
the place of one Mans' suffering
which won us victory, over the plights in life,
trouble and strife,
the battles we fight.

Introducing Jesus Christ Lord and Saviour,
He is the light for a brighter tomorrow.

Lay down your soulish weapons
for a brighter tomorrow,
run to the River of Life
and drown all your sorrow.

The Times We're in Can't be Ignored!

The times we're in cannot be ignored:
the faces behind the masks,
the plight of families behind closed doors.
It's evident on the streets, the highways and
the byways, people passing, anger
and desperation fuelling their faces.
One step forward two paces back,
increased utilities, frustration and hostilities
in the political sphere,
resignations, shame and disgraces,
high-rise tower blocks going up in blazes.
The times we're in are fraught with challenges,
social, economic, political and moral.
Countries, cities towns and nations all round being
ravaged, evidence of a world stage damaged!
The media worldwide reporting bad news,
this channel, that channel adding to woes
and Monday blues.
People everywhere barely keeping minds and
soul together, desperately seeking shelter
from the storms and thunderous strange weather.
Covid-19 and lockdowns, a catalyst for change?
We're all coming to the reality of
never being the same.
The times we're in can be a precipitant for a
brighter day; how can this be, I hear you say?

There is one who is Sovereign,
there is one who is Lord;
there is one in charge of the Earth
who sends out a call to all.

The signs in the heavens above, the weather and
climate change, the evidence played out in lives
below in every tribe, nation city and place.
The times we're in points to Sin from Eden's Garden,
where unfortunately it all began.
Let's all take heart in the Good News past,
Jesus Christ the victor played our part,
so, you and I can win in every season
we find ourselves in.

EMETE OGBOMO

Youth—What Do You See?

What do you see when you look at today's youth?
Your son, your daughter, grandchild, niece or
nephew, relations with brown eyes, hazel or blue.

Young people of every nationality across the globe
who look like me and look like you.
The youth of today have lots to say, they convey
energy, drive and express a diversity of views,
good, bad, indifferent, middle of the road, but,
nevertheless, progressively moving forward
with the freedom to choose.

What they want, what they need is oftentimes
influenced by what they hear and see
in you and in me.

Celebrity influencer, TV personality the many types,
share, share, share, click, click, click...like.
Finger or thumb, use both or use one, the new social
media generation representative in the young.

When we turn our eyes to looking at today's youth,
we should see better, mature, enhanced potential
of a Creator God, brimming with purpose
an ordained life of destiny.

The young are among those destined to succeed,
be propelled and go beyond our achievements
where we are now to excel and exceed!

We have it in our gifting and ability a key to impact
the youth now, and the next generation
to become all they can be. Doctors, nurses,
accountants and singers; technicians, pilots,
scientists, actors and teachers. Athletes, presenters,
pastors or priests, all manner of stars, no bars,
golfers, gardeners and drivers of fast cars!

Does what I say strike a chord?
Supporting the youth, a worthwhile cause.
Let's be a life-changer, a difference-maker;
today's youth, tomorrow's Prime Minister or
President elect, youth from all walks of life
with whom to connect.

Executives, husbands and wives, when you
drill it all down, real people, real lives.
Youthful, young and beautiful make an
investment in their lives, Watch them grow,
develop and progress designed to thrive.

Freedom of choice, freedom to choose, to make a
difference impacting the educational lives of youths.
Let the story unfold in our youth, we behold their
gifts, talents, skills and ability. Education is a key
to unlocking their full potential and capability.

Young people out there listen and be wise,
you're destined for greatness onwards, forward
and keep your eyes on the prize. Look to the skies
there's a creator God who watches over your lives.

Education, Education, Education

Education, Education, Education
what's your vocation?
Education has many faces and will take us many
places, far and wide, progress as you aim high
like an Eagle soaring in the sky.

Education is the building block towards progress
forward and upwards, the achievement of your best.

The best-ever you, the best that you can be,
ground level foundations, certificates, qualifications,
accolades, trophies gold, silver, red, white and blue.

Where education starts career progress takes its
course, whether as a Teacher, Doctor,
Lawyer, Pilot and all variety of sports
education leads the way for your vocation.

The platform for your why, moving high
aiming for the moon and everything
is possible for you.

Education comes in a variation for all cultures,
genders, ages nationalities and nations.
Education empowers the poor by tools
and resources to do more.

For the young education paves the way
for destiny fulfilment, whilst still
having fun and time for play.

Educate and re-educate, unlearn past
negative behaviours, embrace lessons
raise your expectation
the many benefits of education.

Education, expectation, diversification, innovation,
generations past, present and to come
have thrived through it.

Education, education whatever the vocation
let it form the bedrock of your foundation
for progressing a key to excelling,
Education, Education, Education.

Memories, Memoirs, Pictures and Postcards

Memories, memoirs, pictures and postcards,
they all get stored in our minds and hearts
as things of the past.
What we have in the here and now is today!
Yesterday's gone, along with its highs and lows,
when the clock strikes midnight,
the day comes to a close.
The choice is ours as to what we do
with moments in time, let's be wise.
Utilise every second, minute, hour of the day,
live life to its fullness, tomorrow's a brand-new day!
The good that we do in the here and now,
can have future rewards affecting the way
in which we look back at the yesteryears,
in memories, memoirs, pictures and postcards.

A Tidal Wave of Hope

A tidal wave of hope is what the Nations need,
The knowledge of the Love of God breaking forth
as the waters cover the sea.

God is Sovereign

Come thunder, lightning, shower or rain,
the Sovereign Lord remains the same.
His love is constant,
His mercy consistent,
His grace unending and
His Love He's sending to every tribe,
tongue and nation.
This talk of God is not a pack of cards;
with him there is no charade.
People of all ages, creed, nationality and races
come to Him just as you are;
And make haste, no bar, no shame
but much gain
now and in the eternity of Heaven's plane.

EMETE OGBOMO

It's Time for Love

As you turn the page, enjoy the paraphrase of a Love Scripture and picture the beauty and potential of what is true about you.

Phase 3

Radical Love

Hugged By Love

Hugged by Love who died for
you, me and all humanity
when He hung on a cross at Calvary.

The story is told in ancient scriptures of old
of a couple Mary and Joseph,
Heavy with child, travelled far and wide
for a place to rest, abide
and deliver the God child.

Hugged by Love from Heaven above,
saved by grace, received in faith.

Hugged by Love firm and secure, covered in
hope, peace and joy and a love so pure
always present certain and sure.

Hugged by Love, He died on a cross and
rose from the dead and
He's knocking at your door!

Swing wide the gate to your heart and receive
Jesus Christ, it's you He awaits.
Hugged by Love, sent from above.

Love Is...

Love is choice in action,
Jesus Christ demonstrated this at the cross
through his suffering and well-known Passion.

His love was costly, priceless unto death today,
it speaks volumes through his
resurrection from the dead!

God's love is not a feeling that wanes
throughout the day,
it's constant as the dawning
and perfect in every way.

Love is wisdom and there's in wisdom in Love,
made available to all humanity
from God, the Father, above.

It chooses to do right in the midst of a wrong;
it turns the other cheek that's
courageous and strong.

God's love has no end, just like a merry-go-round;
it echoes Agape and Phileo the sounds.

Let love be what we choose to do;
acts of kindness birthed from
a heart full of God's Truth.

Passionate Lover

My God is a passionate lover, who from Heaven
showers us with love like no other.

Such Agape love, as a ring with no end,
the evidence of His love in Jesus Christ
His only son was sent.

Passionate lover, a love so sweet,
pure and holy sweeping me off my feet.

Filling my heart and soul with joy
in awestruck wonder,
my passionate lover I behold.

Passionate lover jealous is his name,
today, yesterday and forever
He's always the same.

Passionate lover available like no other,
twenty-four seven and three six five;
call Him up there's a direct line.

Jesus Christ, he's always on time,
I continue my rhyme.

Make haste to the secret place,
bask in his presence, seek the face
of the passionate lover.

Passionate lover who seeks our highest good,
all powerful and mighty, Jesus Christ is
the lover of my soul in this story being told.

God's love is pure and so sweet,
introducing you to the passionate lover
to meet.

Repent of all sin open your heart and let Him in,
with the passionate lover in your heart,
in life you can only but win.

The Cost of the Cross

The cost of the Cross, the price for a life,
Jesus paid with his blood for you and me.

The cost of the Cross, the price of Love,
sent from the Father in Heaven above.

Jesus Christ paid with his life so that
you and I would enjoy the benefits of his sacrifice.

What height of Love, what depths of peace
when Jesus Christ into our lives do we receive.

His Passion and suffering for all of humanity;
so, in choosing eternal life, one day,
Jesus and the Father we will see.

The cost of the Cross Jesus won, the devil lost,
redemption received, and victory achieved.

The cost of the Cross, Jesus the Saviour,
God the Father, the ultimate Boss.

Radical Love

Radical love, sizzling, bursting at the seams,
sent from GOD in Heaven above.
Radical love so pure, kind, unconditional,
precious and divine.

Radical love sees the best in everyone, apart
from the scars, hurts, warts and all sorts.

Radical love so perfect in essence,
generous in mercy and grace
and yes it makes no sense.

Radical love is blind to colour, status, race, ability,
gender, disability and sex,
it keeps on giving mercy and more
of what we don't expect.

Radical love expects nothing in return,
it keeps on giving more of the good
and it's nothing we can earn.

Let love be the bar, the standard to attain
in loving others unconditionally is empowering
and much more to gain.

Radical love is beyond empathy,
beyond mathematical calculation,
its divine, sublime and infinite at all times!

The Love Walk

I'm doing a Love Walk, come stroll with me;
1st Corinthians 1 and 3 in which we see,
Love is patient, love is kind, long suffering,
hopeful and enduring. All of these things,
all of the time, I continue in this rhyme.

Of the many gifts we pour into others,
Love trumps as the greatest of them all.
It covers all sin; it works from within.
It permeates the deepest recesses
of the soul and has no end.

I chose to walk in the path of Love,
sent from the Father in Heaven above.
God is Love and first loved me, so I choose
to extend that love unconditionally to friends,
enemies, family, frenemies and all humanity.

Love is Always in Season

LOVE is always in season
and Jesus is the reason.
No matter how high
or no matter how low,
love is able to see us through
the winter, spring, summer and
autumn seasons in our lives.
Why?
Because Jesus Christ paid the price
when he shed his precious blood,
gave his life as the ultimate sacrifice
and that's the reason why
LOVE is always in season.

EMETE OGBOMO

A Kiss from Heaven

The Father's love paid in blood,
His only son He gave,
This paved the way for a brand-new day,
a blank page, sin's stain all wiped away.
Jesus Christ sent from above to all humanity,
A gift of love, pure as a dove,
reliable, dependable,
available twenty-four seven,
a priceless and precious
Kiss from Heaven.

Deeper Love

Just as the greatest treasures
are hidden underground,
Just as the way up is down.

Just as in seeking the Lord he will be found,
Just as the earth on all its axis, is round.

Just as the waves of the sea gives sound,
So is the Love of God profound.

Just as the sparkling jewels are in a crown,
Going deeper in God is perfect Love found.

What is Love?

Love is patient love is kind, love does not
keep a record, playback or rewind,
of the things of the past
churned over in the mind.
Love is care, and not a cold stare
conveying how could you dare
Do that, say that!

Love is trait of a believer in Jesus Christ,
because of it He paid the price
For the new life, all sin and transgressions
and wanton rebellion.
Love is the icing on the cake which abates:
hate,
bitterness,
resentment and malice,
unforgiveness,
stagnation and regression.

God's love from above is pure and holy,
everlasting and enduring.
Embrace God's love and be encased all around
and release it to all people of every nation
in a lost and dying world
I choose to love and all that it is.

Loved

I am loved and I love and in loving others
I suffer long.
Love is reflected in respect and kindness
no self-display
and hides from pride.

No rudeness in sight, seeking the
well-being of others,
and not just mum, dad,
sisters and brothers.

Love responds to provocation with hesitation,
challenging negative thinking at a blink.

Love does not delight at the sight
of wrongdoing but holds onto the Truth,
Bearing, believing, enduring
and hopeful in all things;
brimming with and ringing the tune of Love
from God in Heaven above,
Never-ending and unfailing LOVE!

My Love Everlasting

My shining light, my hearts delight;
my peace, my joy and solitude.
My soul and mind, every moment in time,
my love everlasting.

More Love...

Love is choice in action,
devoid of fear, anxiety, hate
and negative reactions.

The Gift of God

The gift of God is Salvation,
The gift of God is love;
The gift of God is kindness to all,
We give glory to the Almighty above.

Phase 4

The Beauty of Salvation

The day Jesus Christ came into my Life!

I remember it well; I remember it clearly:
February 1996 God met me in a state of despair
And showered me with his love so dearly.

> I surrendered my heart to God and
> from then I began to see clearly.

The day God came into my life,
I had no other choice but to give him all I had:
My heart, my mind and soul.

He took me in as a lost sheep,
fed me with milk for weeks and weeks,
Oh, how sweet this did feel,
it marked the beginning of the zeal!

I was a happy bunny filled with joy,
the works of darkness in my life by God's
supernatural power were destroyed.

Things began to happen extraordinarily
to say the least, it was clear you were here,
and I was born again.

I now live an overcoming life in Jesus Christ
because he paid the ultimate price
for my former sinful life.

Introducing Jesus

Introducing Jesus the man of LOVE,
sent by God from heaven above,
pure in spirit, harmless as a dove.

This same Jesus, walked the earth
with purpose and a goal to unite humanity
back to God to heal, deliver, set free
and make whole.

Jesus came to bear the pain of all the ills
we suffer, Jesus came to lift the shame,
the sinful part of our nature.

Let's draw closer to home,
right here and right now,
here's me looking at you,
Godly in image with a body,
spirit and soul.

You are skilfully and wonderfully made,
God breathed the breath of life, uniquely
fashioned to enjoy each and every day.

Jesus came in love to share
the Good News of the Gospel.
Abide in Him so you may win
the gift of your Salvation.

EMETE OGBOMO

The King on a Cross

The King on the cross
paid the cost for the sins of humanity,
The King on the cross
gave his life, the price to save the lost.
The King on the cross
suffered shame and disgrace
death by scourging what could be worse.
The King on the cross
clothes torn, shared, discarded
before a hostile crowd to say the least,
head bowed, blood shed
the price for victory and eternal peace.
For you and for me and
entire families to receive,
introducing Jesus Christ,
The King of all kings who lived
who died and without questions
rose from the grave.
He's alive and coming again!
The King on a cross,
now seated in heaven, the Big Boss
invites all to come in blood,
washed and free from sin and
start over a new spiritual life
and be born again.

The Question of Sin

The question was asked, "What is sin?"
A life separated from the knowledge of God
that resides deep within.
Every man, woman boy and girl, no one is excluded,
blonde hair, blue eyes, dark skin or yellow
we're symptomatically prone to
wanting to do life on terms of our own!
Our nature became corrupted in the
Garden of Eden, back in time.
Adam and Eve to God did cleave,
until evil crept in with the intention to deceive.
Yes, Eve, the Mother of all the living,
eyed the fruit and called on her husband
who joined in the pursuit.
Sin, sin the stain within
guilty as charged
and the penalty it brings.

Jesus Saves

Jesus saves, and life exists beyond the grave.
The grass withers and the flower fades,
Human life is like grass that withers and fades,
there's spiritual life that exists beyond the grave—
Jesus saves.

Jesus came and paved the way for you and me
to be redeemed, to be saved.
Salvation is free for you and for me,
no more a slave to sin, the price paid in blood
on Calvary's tree, the ultimate victory.

Jesus saves, believe me, life exists
beyond the grave.
"How do I benefit?" the question may be.

Open your mouth, believe in your heart
and pray this prayer with me:
Lord Jesus thank you for dying for me,
I am a lost soul standing repentant before thee.
Forgive my sins and fill me
with your Holy spirit to be born again.

God of the Morning

God of the morning, my early delight,
God of the morning, peaky and bright.
God of the morning, the first one to greet
God of the morning, the Holy Spirit so sweet.

God in the morning, my heart to engage,
God in the morning, the Ancient of days!

God in the morning, whose face to seek,
earnestly waiting, expectant and meek.
God in the morning, I need more of you,
direction, encouragement, healing, counsel,
my portion of Truth.

God in the morning, new mercies I see,
the unfailing words in Lamentations 3:23.
You are God of the morning and my song at night,
come manifest your goodness, power, presence,
Display to all around to see,
as I go and carry and shine your light.
God of the morning, good morning.

EMETE OGBOMO

Sold-Out Lover

Sold-out lover, I'll never give myself to another,
Lord I'm a sold-out lover.
I'm wholly devoted to you in all that I do,
in all that I am, in all that I can do,
through Jesus your Son and
soon again, coming King.

Sold-out lover, I'm God's special treasure
called, equipped and covered. Committed at the
core, having no other, I'm a sold-out lover to God.

Through the hurt and through the pain
in devotion to worship, there is much gain.
Sold-out lover putting God first,
priority and hunger for you do I thirst.

Sold-out lover, the Lord is generous in grace,
jealous is His name, give him his pride of place
and honour due to his name!

Sold-out lovers commanded to worship,
take time to pour adoration on the King,
Give him Lordship, invite him in.

Sold-out lovers fall in love with Jesus all over again
and receive an abundance of divine Godly rain.

Home!

Home! A place to call your own,
a place of rest, relaxation a zone
of comfort where you welcome your guests.
Home! Where you are never alone!
A place of solitude where we're free
to display all kinds of attitudes.
Home! The place where you're known
and the person that you are, and maybe
not the personality that others see from afar!
Home! Where you can be in your zone,
yet surprisingly still feel alone.
So, what is home for you?
A home for me is a place of peace free from strife,
Where I and my loved ones enjoy
all social aspects of everyday life.
You and yours, mother, brother, dad, sister, niece,
nephew uncle aunty and lover,
lest I forget any other.
Home alone was Macaulay Culkin,
mum and dad the other side of the world
leaving thieves to break in.
He did a good job of defending the home
with fun, humour and laughs,
yet the thieves would not leave him alone.
Then there's the phrase:
An English man's home is his castle;
dare you trespass over the threshold?

Can I be controversial with a statement of faith
so as not to offend? I will put forward my own case!
February 1996, depressed and suicidal, life's not
moving forward and I felt lost and bone idle.
In my depression I arose without hesitation to a
regular church near Clapham Station.
I ran in as a big mess, angry, frustrated, teary-eyed
and in my soul no rest.
But I came out with a shout of joy in my heart,
happiness in my step,
In those few minutes with God,
I met who leads me home, to Jesus Christ,
which changed the trajectory of my entire life.

No Glory Without a Story

There's no glory without the story,
no victory without the Cross,
no peace without the Prince of it,
Jesus Christ came to win the lost.
He paid the price as a sacrifice
his precious blood the cost.

Jesus—The Fountain of Living Water

The fountain of Living Waters,
springs upon springs upon springs,
overflowing abundant joy with all
the goodness that it brings.

Fountain of Living Waters, flowing
from Heaven above, waters so pure
to an allure to heart and soul,
issues receive every cure.

Fountain of Living Water running
deeper than the eyes can see,
so vast its mass so great its reach
channels of refreshing, reviving and
blessing hungry souls to meet.

The fountain of Living Waters,
God incarnate, the blessed Truth.

Fountain of Living Waters flowing
endlessly from mountain peaks to the
valley lows, nations, places and cities
gushing unceasingly through the streets.

The fountain of living waters is flowing your way,
come jump in mother, brother, father, sister,
daughter, nephew and niece,
surrender your life to Jesus Christ today
and receive never-ending peace!

Simply the Cross

Thank you for the Cross, that you, for the cost paid;
the life, you gave for all humanity so that we may
receive new life now and eternally.

Thank you for the Cross, you're the Boss, the
Creator of all things. Almighty, victorious ruling and
reigning in sovereignty throughout all the earth
now and after the final bell rings.

The Cross speaks, the Cross meets
every human need, for rich and poor, young or old
and somewhere in between.

God's redemptive plan for sinful humanity,
Jesus Christ the atoning sacrifice paid the price
with his blood and life, so that you and I
can make the choice to live in freedom,
no condemnation, full of joy and peace.

To be used by a Holy God to bring a change,
make a difference the constancy of
God's love and assurance.

Come to the Cross, lay down all your loss
and pick up a brand new you.
The Father's love sent from above, Jesus Christ,
pure and Holy, the Life and Living Truth.

I have a Confession to Make!

I have a confession to make,
I am engaged in a love affair that's not out there,
nor subject to wear and tear.

It's centred within the core of my being,
it radiates with joy and ensuing peace, no grease
or grime, acidity, lemon or lime.

Time after time, I experience a glow, no show,
display or array, no pomp or ceremony,
It's just me and Him, three encompassed in one:
Holy Spirit, Father and Son.

I'm engaged in a love affair that extends to
majestic heights, located in the heavenly realms
but experienced through the courtship of God's
unfailing light. Jesus Christ is the lover of my soul
in this story being told.

I am engaged in a love affair; you are invited
if you dare; Come to the River of Life,
you will find healing there and begin your own
personal relational love affair.

I have a confession to make, there's no mistake,
Jesus Christ can make you whole and
give you a new story in his sight to behold.
I have a confession to make!

EMETE OGBOMO

The Goodness of God

The goodness of God, lest we forget,
in the morning I arose, at night-time I slept.
The goodness of God, each day, fresh
in the morning, new mercies flood my way.

The goodness of God avails like a flood,
whooshing towards me abundant in Love.
The goodness of God surrounds me on every side
wherever I go his presence still abides.

The goodness of God to me, the sacrificial love
paid in blood, hung on a tree called Calvary.
The goodness of God, from heaven above, avails
to humanity an abundance of unconditional Love.

Love that's unconditional, unwavering and kind;
the type that keeps giving in all seasons of life.

The goodness of God cannot be ignored,
it's moving, hovering, knocking at your door.
It's packaged in good things to enjoy in this life
by you and by me, God's goodness is divine.

God Most High

There's no high like the Most-High God,
mighty in power located beyond the sky
in Heaven above.
There's no drug or medication no alcoholic drink,
fast car, sky dive, which can take you higher,
in exhilaration beyond your soul, bringing joy
to your spirit where you thrive.
There's no God like the Most-High God Creator
of it all: man, woman, boy, girl
and on earth below, every colour race and
nationality depicted in the rainbow.
There's no high like God Most High
glorious and Holy loving, faithful and kind.
There's no high like the Most-High
who hears every cry, sees every tear
in his omnipresence.

Jesus, I Love You

Jesus, I love you, you're everything I need.
Jesus, I love you, you meet my every need.
Into my life you came, saved, planted the seed
that lit the flame,
giving rise to the Power of God
in Jesus's name.

Christ my Satisfaction

Only Jesus Christ can satisfy the deep longings
and desires of the human soul.
Only in Him can we be cleansed, be fulfilled
and made whole.

Christ, the one who can fill us up
to running over an overflowing cup.

When we are empty, when we are down,
He can lift our head, He is our crown.
Clothed in his glory power and strength,
all of our days, let Christ be the length.

Christ, our satisfaction, the length of our days,
today, yesterday and forever He's always the same.

Jesus Christ the living Truth,
sacrificed his life for me and for you.
Christ, our satisfaction above all else,
in our heart, he deserves first place.

The Antidote

The antidote to rejection is God's acceptance.
Lack of ability to cope, God's hope.
The blame game, freedom from shame.

The antidote for offence is love without condition.
The cure for insecurity is Christ-like identity.

The answer to self-harm, the blood of Jesus,
the complete healing balm.
The remedy for timidity, a sound mind,
God's power and ability.

The solution for imperfection,
Jesus's resurrection.

The answer to eternal death is Salvation;
so, hasten knock at the door
receive new life through Jesus Christ
and live forevermore—it's the full cure.

Going for God!

I'm going for God, looking above
taking hold of that for which Jesus Christ
died for me, the price paid in blood at Calvary.

I'm running towards the mark, to attain the goal,
pursuing perfection through the holiness of God.

I'm journeying with the Lord in the heavens above,
keeping my eyes on the prize,
filled with his gift of love.

Jesus Christ, the lover of my soul, called me
from darkness into marvellous light
and has made me whole.

I'm a candidate for Heaven, bound for glory,
journeying through life, fulfilling purpose
and impacting lives.

Filled with compassion for the downtrodden souls,
reaching out to as many young ones,
poor, rich and old.

Demonstrating God's love and power, no limits
no barrier to reach fallen humanity
with Jesus my strength.

I'm going for God and there's no looking back;
no turning, no swerving left or right.

I'm sticking to the course laid out for me,
brimming with purpose impacting lives,
making a difference to humanity.

Each day that I rise, I fix my eyes,
looking to the skies, focused on the prize
of eternity.
I'm going for God, come journey with me
to pursue purpose and fulfil destiny.

EMETE OGBOMO

You and God—Where Are You?

January, February, March, April then May,
where are you in your relationship with God today?

Yes, dear friend, with the maker of it all,
where are you standing?
Long, short, somewhere in the middle or tall?

You and God—where are you?

Sound familiar? I remind us of God's question to
the first creation, Adam, and first woman, Eve,
the originators of the Father's plan.

It's not without question that God knew
where they were, in his omnipresence here,
there and everywhere.

So, then why the question from the
knower of all things? Answer: there's
a revelatory insight that God wanted to bring.

Adam and Eve were God breathed
and man became a living soul, spiritually perfect
at one with God and made whole.

They walked in unison, naked in birth clothing,
there was no fault in them no embarrassment
of nothing to be ashamed.

They played in the Garden as husband and wife,
living amongst the animals and
all forms of lush plant life.

Then one day, Eve's eye turned away and looked
upon a fruit that maybe she saw every day.

The Tree of Knowledge, of good and evil was
the devil's bait; it came subtly knocking,
suggesting appealing to Eve's eye-gate.

Hey, all that fruit sure looks good.
Where my boo at? We sure got to try that!

Adam, her man, also fell for the bait, despite
God's command to him that you must not eat!

The serpent's plan strengthened as they both agree;
let's eat the fruit and see what we can be.

Like gods, the serpent said, you will become,
in the day that you eat of it, like the
Most High and Holy One.

Of course, this was a lie from the pit of hell, when
they ate of the fruit all of humanity fell,
Spiritually from God and vast disconnect, the result
of one man's sin, what did they expect?

There is only one God, the Creator of it all,
who sent his son Jesus to pay the debt for us all.
The price for sin that resides deep within,
the nature of our being

Jesus Christ shed his blood, rose from the dead
for you and me to be spiritually born again.
Back to the question of
where are you (me) with God?

I'm ultra, super-duper desperate for more of Him
every day, in every way to live, breathe,
move and have my being like
an ongoing song to be singing.

God, You're Amazing

God, you're amazing, unto you will I keep gazing.
Lifting my eyes to the skies, the beauty, splendour
and magnificence of God.

Lord, you're amazing, truly amazing, no mistaking
the depth of your love.
The height of your faithfulness that reaches
the heavens, the perfection encapsulated
in the number seven.

Lord, you're amazing my heart is blazing with
unspeakable joy and love immeasurable,
The work of your Spirit, pure, Holy and true;
such an amazing God let all come unto you.

EMETE OGBOMO

Where Will You Go?

Where will you go
when you breathe your last breath?
Will your soul make it
to the place of eternal rest?
Will you go up or will you go down
make no mistake spiritual life
exists beyond the ground!

Whether you're cremated
or buried in the ground,
eternity awaits the human spirit
before the pearly gates
each one of us will stand.
We will all appear before God,
the Creator of life and account for our lives,
so fleeting just like a vapour in the wind.
Heaven is the place of eternal rest,
freedom from pain, no striving, no stress.

Heaven, dear friend, is as real as it comes,
eternal enjoyment for boys, girls, friends, dads,
mums, your chums, bestie and all the rest whoever,
walk or run just make the decision to come
and not be left behind.

The Blood of Jesus Christ

The blood of Jesus does wonders and speaks volumes in all stages of life!
The blood of Jesus atoned for the sins of the world and all of humankind.

EMETE OGBOMO

Phase 5

The Wonders of Faith

The Good News is You!

The Good News concerns you;
the Good News is yours,
your choice to pursue your God-given destiny
surrounded by heavenly applause.
The heroes of faith and the example they left;
Abraham believed God against all hope
that Sarah would bear a child
despite her womb being dead!
What about Esther called to be a Queen,
risked her life for a nation
in asking out of season
to speak with the King.
You recall Joseph, enslaved into
prison captivity, but against all the odds
conducted himself with integrity,
receiving favour from God.
Then there's Daniel in the lion's den
(a God-fearing man with integrity),
who chose to be unfazed by the threat of death
and prayed twenty-four-seven instead.
There are more, but I chose these four
to convey the truth that applies to you,
In common with them,
the choice to move forward
by faith in God is up to you.
We experience life in seasons,
sometimes highs and lows,
time spent in the middle

when you simply don't know
what's going on what's it all about,
frustrations, inhalation just want to let out a shout!
Well, it occurred to me the other day,
God chose to bring you and me
to this earth for a reason,
purpose and season
this life as we know it
can be ever so fleeting.
It was out of our hands to determine.
Therefore, with faith in hand
we can choose to turn over
to him the reins of our heart,
The fears that we have as to
what the future holds,
like the heroes of faith,
be courageous and bold.
Determine to embrace
the season you're in,
pursue the God of Heaven for
your life and you can only but win!
Turn your mess into a message,
in your shame there is much gain.
If the whole world is a stage,
then you and I are actors
with the opportunity to
turn over a fresh page each day.
The Good News is yours to choose.

Faith: Certain and Sure

Faith is not a feeling but an action much like a verb,
it requires an activity in response to a spoken word.
What is that prompting you have in your heart to go
in a particular direction to play your active part;
just as the author poised with ink and pen write,
just as the turtle hibernates for winter out of sight,
just as the swimmer, ready to dive,
just as a predator hunts to survive,
just as the golfer, ready to swing,
just as a bird to fly raises its wings,
just as a soprano ready to sing.
Do you have promises from God that remain
outstanding and yet to come to pass?
By faith believe, with gratitude receive,
with certainty and hope get on the move
and groove your way without hesitation
into the manifestation.

Faith: Heaven's Currency

Step into the Red Sea and it will part for me.
By faith approaching, fully assured
equipped and chosen.

God's good pleasure, His perfect will;
embrace the challenge
advance and be still.

See the Lord's deliverance
that He gives on the way, grace and mercy
affirmations declared for every day.

Never mind the how and when,
stand on God's promises
he's faithful to the end.

My knees do I bend, the word I sow as the seed
to meet the need, I pass through the sea;
the waters recede on the banks of the river and
fulfilment of the vision the promises achieved—
mission accomplished!

EMETE OGBOMO

Keys to Faith

Faith is the key and the currency of Heaven
to activate God's promises and blessing
twenty-four seven.

Yes, you can scream and shout,
wriggle and shake all over and about.
But the key, to see the manifestation from Heaven,
is faith.

Faith cannot falter, fail or fade;
faith saved Moses from death on the Nile.
Faith is full of hope, being certain and sure,
that what God said he would do
will come knocking at your door.

Faith is the currency by which Abraham believed
the determining factor by which Sarah conceived.

By faith you and I can move a mountain
standing in our way, just speak like Joshua,
the sun stands still this day!

Faith is like the charger that reconnects
the mobile device, the battery to power up believing,
reaching Heaven and God beyond the skies.

By faith, God created the Heavens,
sky, sea and earth by the power of His Word.
Faith is sight beyond the skies and
looking to God, Jehovah Jireh to provide.

The Faith Connection

The whole world is a stage,
day by day presents a new page,
Another chance and another opportunity,
another moment to seize our eternal destiny.
What might that be?
What might I see?
What can I do to take hold of the life
God has prepared and ordained for me?
Faith is the key.

I can see clearly now my sin has gone;
I can move closer to God through his Son, Jesus,
whose life was spent on a Cross called Calvary,
upon his death and resurrection
it brought new life for you and me.

What a wonder, what an amazement,
what an opportunity to seize an engagement
with your eternal destiny,
by receiving and embracing God's love,
it's a case of believing and receiving.

Come on, be brave and enter God's Kingdom stage
and begin a new page,
come to the river of life and be **SAVED!**

Faith Is...

Faith is as certain as an anchor is secure.
Faith sees that thing in the here and now,
knocking at the door.
Faith is the walk that supports the talk.
Faith is action, not distraction, retraction or doubt,
certain assurance of end goal worked out!
Faith is the key that opens the door
to manifest promises of God and so much more.
Faith, the confidence of certainty and hope that says,
"Yes, I believe you Lord
your word is Truth
of this, I am sure."

Faith Talk

By faith believe it,
by faith receive it,
by faith step out
and take hold of it!
Leave no room for doubt,
lift up your voice
with declarations and
affirmations of victory.
When the Word of God comes
with your whole heart, believe it,
with assurance receive it
and by faith act upon it!

Faith Sees

Faith sees, faith believes, faith conceives
the promise of that hoped for,
Faith is the key that opens the door.

Faith surrounds itself with the evidence of hope,
an expectation and manifestation
Of what, when and how...

Hope is a sight of a desired future thing;
faith is the vehicle from Heaven to earth
That brings the promise in—
time for that victory sing.

Faith Takes Action

Faith is an attitude with actionable steps,
it believes and sees the result of what it expects.

"What eyes have seen, what ears have heard,
what God has prepared for those who love him",
says <u>1 Corinthians 2:9</u>
We need only believe
the truth of what He speaks.

Phase 6

Kingdom Living

The Kingdom Within

The Kingdom within, no more am I
a captive slave to sin.
Blood washed, purchased and purified
by Christ the King.

The Kingdom within Christ's power,
rule and reign,
invariably and undoubtably life will
never be the same.

The old has gone, it's in with the new,
manifestation of change is up or down to you!

The Kingdom within God's image displayed
through us here on earth,
from the beauty and wonder of the
spiritual rebirth.

Not physical or natural but spiritual
by the Holy Ghost, supernatural.

The Kingdom, within means an abundance
of joy and happiness
overwhelming, the devil is defeated,
and God's children excelling.

Advancing in power, strength and might,
wielding the Word of God as a sword
and shining forth God's light to a lost generation.

Battling tribulations and woes,
Jesus came to set free
and release the helpless and lost souls.

The Kingdom within contains all
that we need,
all things for life and godliness was given
to Abraham's seed.

So, let's be bold, let's take hold
of the Kingdom within and reign with him,
Christ Jesus, our ever-present, soon-coming King.

You're Amazing

When you look in the mirror what do you see?
Confess, profess, affirm or express?

I am amazing in all that I see,
fearfully and wonderfully made
in God's perfection, reflection and imagery.

It is written in the Book, come let's take a look:
Psalms 139 and 14, each and every line,
That my soul knows full well, praises to God
for his intricate handiwork
my innermost being,
my every cell.

So, now when you look in the mirror,
affirm, confess, profess and express;
I'm God's best and greatness
resides on the inside of me,
It's time to align with God's picture of me,
filled with the power of God destined to succeed.
I'm God's best, made in his image;
called, anointed, appointed to fulfil destiny,
yes that's me!

There's no mistaking, you are amazing!

Good News for You!

Ambassadors for Christ demonstrate,
emulate his light day and night,
in the sight of all to see.
Christ Ambassadors, yes, you and that's me.

We, who belong to Him that sing
the redemption song, be strong
in the Lord and the power of His might.
Advancing His kingdom burning with Holy fire,
pushing back the darkness
with ever-increasing light.

Ambassadors for Christ called by God,
anointed and appointed,
living stones and epistles
to be read by men, women, boys and girls,
humanity's gaze is upon us
north, east, south and west.

Christ Ambassadors is it any wonder
why God chose you to carry the Good News?
Rhetorically said, make no mistake,
pre-destined and selected vessels
of honour set apart,
Holy the potter's art to shine forth
His glory to share with the world
redemption story.

Ambassadors for Christ called to a life
of sacrifice a call to bring Heaven's peace
and for hatred to cease.

Let kindness bind us and anger take a back seat.
Patience with friends and enemies included,
pride and boasting amongst the things excluded.
Then there's love that sets the stage and scene,
Ambassador for Christ filled with new life,
go forth and serve our King.
Christ Ambassadors, you and me shining,
Christ's light burning bright
impacting fallen humanity.
Christ Ambassadors, a privilege and honour
to serve the King of Kings,
now and forever.

INSPIRED FOR PURPOSE

You're One of a Kind

You're one a kind, there's no one like you,
Gorgeous, handsome, beautiful, special,
intricately crafted, fully protected
in your mother's womb.

Your eyes, whether hazel, brown, green or blue,
no one else has them, they're unique to you.
Of your ears, nose and mouth, the same is true.
Your mind, soul, body and spirit beautifully created
by God made in his image.

You're filled with potential, residual source of power
to carry out exploits aided by supernatural power.

Be not defined by failure, be not defined by lack,
be not defined by the opinions of others
no captive slave to the past.

Be not defined by bad experiences from the past,
momentary happenings, such seasons will pass.

You're one of a kind, jewel in a crown, a rare find.
You are called to greatness, set apart,
born to win and called to shine.

EMETE OGBOMO

Life of the Sunny Side

Life on the sunny side, Kingdom-living kingdom life:
Free from worry, free from strife.

Life on the sunny side where you're free;
achieve purpose and fulfil destiny.
Life of the sunny side, the world is your oyster,
come live your best life.

Life on the sunny side is full of joy, peace and
happiness beyond measure forever.
Draw near to the allure of the sunny side of life,
it's free to enter through Jesus, the door
who paid the price.

He hung on a Cross for you and for me;
He died and rose from the dead
to set all humanity free.
From a life full of fear and despair to cast every
burden onto him and find healing there.

The sunny side of life is available to all who
call on the name of Jesus Christ and
receive him as Lord.
Lord of your life from now and until he comes again
to take his children to their eternal heavenly home.

Life of the sunny side come on over receive
the free gift of Love like a four-leaf Clover.

Time for a Reset!

Truth is, along life's road, life happens to us,
and we can get stuck!
Yes, often-times we are down on our luck.
If you are to continue in well-being and relevance,
here's the good news, you need to get a RESET!
Whether transitioning childhood, youth,
adulthood or legacy dreams,
All are possible, no matter how difficult it seems.

What's in the RESET, what can you expect?
Repair, remake, alteration and remodelling.
Replanning, rehabilitation,
conversion and restoration.
Reorganise, reform, regenerate and remake!

Several dimensions of wellness in life,
human's spirit, body and mind, tripartite beings.
Mental, physical, social, vocational,
emotional and spiritual.
Elimination of limitations, fear, doubts
and unconscious programming,
broken record syndrome.
Misaligned relationships and identity mismatch.

How to get unstuck?
Stop, think, decide, shift and clear, action, routine
action will all get you there!
With a RESET, you win—let the shift begin.

EMETE OGBOMO

Live a Life of Purpose

Live a life of purpose,
despite the swings and roundabouts,
ups and downs and sometimes a circus.
Purposed by design are you,
special unique and one a kind.

Yes, it is true in all the world
there's no one like you.
Your face, features, hair colour and skin,
all that's on the outside
and uniquely fashioned within.

Like time invested deeply woven tapestry,
intricate and delicate, body, soul and spirit.
Your life has a purpose the Why for your being,
the beautiful plan that exists with
lifted eyes for your seeing.

There's a reason for your existence,
a reason why you are here,
like the purpose of oxygen
unseen but littering the air,
your life has meaning with a
worthwhile contribution
to humanity to share.

Destiny is calling through the pathway of purpose,
you're created for good works beyond the 9-5,
superficially religious and all that lip service.

Your life has meaning, value and worth,
there's an original calling to benefit mother earth!
Be Inspired for purpose and wired for life!

The Best is Yet to Come...

Receive this big shout out, be in no doubt,
The Best is Yet to Come.

The best for you, what you can do,
achievements, fulfilling your purpose,
your why for living and that's the truth.

Believe it or not you're called to greatness,
set apart to run life's race, to be the best ever you,
destined for a God goal and receive
all the goodness that's due.

By faith believe,
The Best is Yet to Come!

Phase 7

Affirmation Time

"I am" Statements of Truth

EMETE OGBOMO

INSPIRED FOR PURPOSE

LIFE

1. I am inspired for purpose and excelling in life.
2. I am an uncommon achiever.
3. I am empowered to be an encourager.
4. I am fruitful and flourish in my exploits and pursuits.
5. I am a well-watered garden and intentional about my spiritual growth.
6. I am moving forward with a transformational mindset.
7. I am advancing in God's plans for my life maximising every moment.
8. I am aligned with God's plan for my life.
9. I am flying high, pioneering like an eagle.
10. I am destined to succeed, excelling at God's supernatural speed.
11. I am called to accomplish God's purpose for my life.
12. I am running the race of life from a place of victory in Christ.
13. I am successfully navigating the challenges in life through Jesus Christ.
14. I am on the winning side with Christ Jesus on my side leading the way.

15. I am a catalyst for change impacting lives with God's goodness.

16. I am fruitful and multiply on all sides.

17. I am journeying through life with God directing my steps, so I win!

18. I am journeying through life on God's pathway illuminated with light.

19. I am destined for greatness focused of Godly goals for my life.

20. I am productive, impactful and successful in the work of my hands.

21. I am rich and abundant in Godly blessings.

22. I am diligent in the works of my hands fulfilling God's plan for my life.

23. I am an achiever through Christ.

24. I am filled with faith and take the corresponding action.

25. I am diligent, dutiful living a purposeful life.

LOVED AND BLESSED

1. I am unconditionally loved by God, and I love without reciprocity.
2. I am motivated by Love as an agent and catalyst for change.
3. I am blessed beyond measure God's special treasure, and He delights in me.
4. I am abandoned to God's love for me
5. I am who God says I am without apology, joy-filled and happy.
6. I am encouraged by God's unconditional love for me.
7. I am blessed by God who delights in me.
8. I am a woman blessed beyond measure, God's special treasure he delights in me.
9. I am totally accepted by God and walk in the confident assurance of his love.
10. I am redeemed by Jesus's death, blood and resurrection without exception.
11. I am assured of God's promises coming to pass in my life, He is faithful.
12. I am accepted by God and loved beyond measure.
13. I am God's special treasure, and He delights in me.

14. I am hidden in the person of Truth, Jesus Christ and live an abundant life.
15. I am strong in God Almighty whose power resides in me.
16. I am a Kingdom builder, wealth creator and expectant receiver.
17. I stand tall with confidence in Christ to do all things excelling in life.
18. I am righteous, holy and blameless before God without fault.
19. I am a Truth carrier, light barer and I choose to make a difference.
20. I am a bride in Christ and licenced to shine at all times.
21. I am bought with a price the precious blood or life of Jesus Christ.
22. I am wealthy and rich with God's love to overflowing.
23. I am encouraged by God's love for me and extend the same to all humanity.
24. I am surrounded by God's goodness, grace love and mercy.
25. I am walking in the divine love of God that knows no bounds.

KINGDOM LIVING

1. I am Kingdom minded and wired for successful living.
2. I am called by God to fulfil purpose.
3. I am a transformational advocate impacting lives towards positive change.
4. I am free from sin cleansed within; there are no chains holding me.
5. I am walking in divine destiny with daily expectancy to succeed.
6. I am an Ambassador for Christ shining forth his Light.
7. I am living in victory, pursing goals expectantly, fulfilling destiny.
8. I am blessed in God's presence and receive favour from the King.
9. I am a light carrier and kingdom advancer.
10. I am my beloved and He is mine, called out of darkness into his glorious light to shine.
11. I am marked with the King's signet ring of the Holy Spirit and shine.
12. I am special, unique set apart and favoured by God.
13. I am endued, infused with power from God Almighty to do great exploits.

14. I am part of a royal priesthood and destined to succeed.
15. I am spiritually free to pursue God's plan for me.
16. I am Kingdom Ambassador commissioned to shine.
17. I am free in Jesus Christ and walking in freedom.
18. I am a child of the King of kings, so in life I win.
19. I am a daughter of the King, so in life I win.
20. I am called, appointed and anointed by God to fulfil destiny and purpose.
21. I am filled with joy from the Lord giving me supernatural strength.
22. I am used by God to impact lives positively every day in all spheres of life.
23. I am enabled by the Holy Spirit to carry out supernatural exploits.
24. I am standing on the Solid Rock of Jesus Christ and have victory in the storm.
25. I am a full citizen among God's people.

SPIRITUAL QUALITIES

1. I am intentional about my spiritual growth and feast on the Word daily.
2. I am the salt of the earth illuminating supernatural light (in the world) for all to see and experience.
3. I am fervent in prayer and persist until I break through.
4. I am like Mount Zion and cannot be moved as I trust in the Lord.
5. I am light in a dark place illuminating God's goodness and radiance.
6. I am in good health and my soul prospers.
7. I am clothed in righteousness and dressed for success.
8. I am radiance in a dark place illuminating God's glory.
9. I am a shining light, burning bright radiating for all to see.
10. I am transformed daily by renewing of my mind on God's Truth. *[Romans 12:2]*
11. I am persistent in prayer and continue until I see manifestation.
12. I am a glory carrier to the nations. *[Matthew 5:13,14]*
13. I am more than a conqueror and an instrument of honour.

14. I am amongst those who fear God and meditate on His name. *[Malachi 3:16]*

15. I am uniquely and wonderfully made. [Psalm 139:14]

16. I am complete in Christ Jesus and there's no flaw in me.

17. I am an intercessor, watchful, alert and discerning.

18. I am strengthened in faith fully assured of God's promises coming to pass in my life.

19. I am super infused with God's power through the Holy Spirit.

20. I am more than capable and more than a conqueror in Jesus Christ. *[Romans 8 :37]*

21. I am a God chaser in endless pursuit of his plans for my life.

22. I am reconciled to God through Christ Jesus. *[Romans 5:10]*

23. I am discreet and sensitive to the Holy Spirit and armed with Truth.

24. I am standing on the firm foundation of Jesus Christ the Rock of my Salvation.

25. I am a worshipper, warrior and encourager.

GODLY VIRTUES

1. I am patient bearing with others and kind.
   [1 Corinthians 13:4]
2. I am merciful, kind and considerate to all.
3. I am valiant and secure in Christ Jesus.
4. I am walking in the fear of God, hating evil and loving good.
5. I am humble, calm, walking in God's peace.
6. I am bought with a price.
7. I am compassionate and well thought of.
8. I am patient, truthful and honest.
9. I am moving hight in the Lord.
10. I am unmovable, unshakable standing on the solid rock of Jesus Christ.
11. I am an overcomer running the race of life from a place of victory.
12. I am growing in Christ.
13. I am learning daily, discerning and justified.
14. I am childlike, set apart and walk in humility.
15. I am a woman of God called and qualified to do exploits.
16. I am a woman of virtue.

17. I am a man of purpose living the God life with intentionality.
18. I am agreeable, merciful, grateful and thankful.
19. I am hopeful, thoughtful.
20. I am in Jesus and Jesus is in me and I shine His light for all to see.
21. I am clothed in righteousness, sanctified and blessed.
22. I am favoured by the King of kings walking in the light of God.
23. I am respectful and respected.
24. I am God's elect chosen to fulfil purpose.
25. I am set apart for the Lord and serve people with joy.

DRESSED FOR SUCCESS

1. I am shining brighter and brighter clothed in majestic glory.
2. I am clothed in honour, alert filled with the Holy Spirit.
3. I am fashioned by God's hands yielded to His plan for my life.
4. I am gifted, blessed and dressed in God's glory for success.
5. I am blessed in the works of my hands fulfilling God's plan for my life.
6. I am crucified with Christ living in the fullness of a resurrected life.
7. I am clothed in God's strength, glory, splendour, virtues, victory and dignity.
8. I am a servant of God.
9. I am the head and stand tall moving higher in my purpose.
10. I am living out the Truth of God's word in every area of my life.
11. I am being conformed to the character of Jesus Christ.
12. I am seen by God a Holy as blameless.
13. I am sealed with the Holy Spirit.
14. I am walking in the fear of the God.

15. I am what the Bible says I am.
16. I am refreshed in God's presence watered by the Truth of the Word.
17. I am covered by God with pinions of light.
18. I am a new creation no longer living in condemnation. [Romans 8:1]
19. I am a royal daughter and all glorious within. [Psalm 45:13]
20. I am because God is, I can do all things because Jesus Christ paid the price for my sin.
21. I am a soul winner sharing the Good News of Salvation everywhere.
22. I am intentional about achieving my goals.
23. I am a carrier of God's glory and favour surrounds me on all sides.
24. I am walking in expectancy on the narrow path fulfilling destiny.
25. I am redeemed and esteemed by God and walk talk with Christ in me.
26. I am bought with a price and enabled through Christ Jesus to do all things.
27. I am light in a dark place running the race of life to receive the eternal prize.
28. I am glorious within, victorious in battle.

About The Author

Emete Ogbomo is a Lawyer and Transformational Advocate, who encourages and inspires others to fulfil destiny and live a purpose filled life, buttressed by her faith in God.

EMETE OGBOMO

INSPIRED FOR PURPOSE

About PublishU

PublishU is transforming the world of publishing.

PublishU has developed a new and unique approach to publishing books, offering a three-step guided journey to becoming a globally published author!

We enable hundreds of people a year to write their book within 100-days, publish their book in 100-days and launch their book over 100-days to impact tens of thousands of people worldwide.

The journey is transformative, one author said,

"I never thought I would be able to write a book, let alone in 100 days... now I'm asking myself what else have I told myself that can't be done that actually can?'"

To find out more visit
www.PublishU.com

Printed in Great Britain
by Amazon